ALLAN HOLDSWORTH

JUST FOR THE CURIOUS

Transcriptions by Hemme Luttjeboer
Additional Text by Aaron Stang
Editor: Aaron Stang
Cover Design: Debbie Johns Lipton
All Photos Courtesy: Glen La Ferman

Copyright © 1993
Beam Me Up Music, c/o CPP/Belwin, Inc.
15800 N.W. 48th Avenue, Miami, FL 33014

Special thanks to Aaron Stang for
his contributions, understanding and creativity.

Foreword

This book is intended to accompany, and perhaps clarify, some of the points in the video.

In my own system, scales do not have names or modes; they have symbols, as I do not think of any scales as having beginnings or endings. The names given in the book are the closest that could be derived from the symbols that I use.

There are of course mind-boggling numbers of scales (and chords that come from them) that are not touched upon in this book or video. I have tried to outline what I would consider the basic and most practical forms with regard to improvising over chord sequences.

This is simply a keyhole glimpse at the way I have come to view harmony – a purely personal way – and likely of no use to others. Therefore, this really is... "Just for the Curious".

Allan Holdsworth

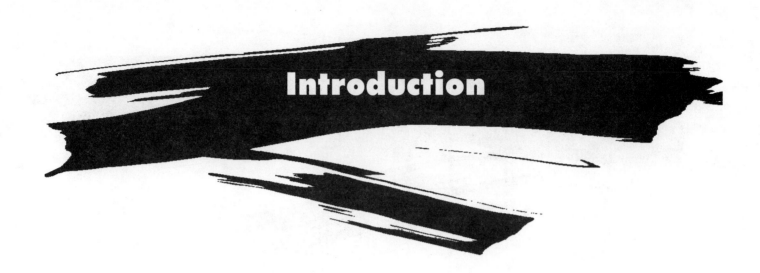

Introduction

To most of us, Allan Holdsworth represents the true, unbridled, creative spirit – always searching and exploring; constantly expanding the boundaries and setting new limits. From his breathtaking legato solos to his beautiful, orchestral solo guitar style (check out Zone on the included recording) he always leaves us asking, "How did he do it; where did he get those chords?"

In this book, Allan sets us on the right road, although the answers are never easy and there is no quick fix, he reveals the basic simplicity and logic of his approach; which is so often misunderstood when we try to define it in terms of traditional music theory: triads, cycles of fourths, etc. Those of you interested in looking at the guitar from a refreshingly new perspective, Allan wrote this for you – "Just for the Curious."

Aaron Stang
Editor

Part I
Scales for Improvising

In this section, Allan discusses the scales he finds most useful for improvisation. It is important that once you become familiar with these scale fingerings that you begin to explore them for all of the chords contained within each. You can do this by building chords from each scale tone.

In most respects Allan is self-taught. He began his exploration of scales by working out various scale patterns and then experimenting with each of their permutations, discarding those with more than four consecutive semi-tones (half-steps). He then analyzed the scales to find the chords contained within them (more on Allan's approach to harmony in Part II).

The following scales will be covered in this section. Although there are many more scales than presented here, these are the most useful. The scales are named in relation to the chord forms and chord tones they imply.

Seven Note Scales:
Scale #1) C Major/D Minor/G7
Scale #2) D Minor (maj7) - (D Melodic Minor)
Scale #3) A Minor (maj7,♭6) - (A Harmonic Minor)
Scale #4) A Minor (maj7,♯4) - (E Harmonic Major)
Scale #14) C Dominant (♯9)

Added Tone "Jazz" Scales (Eight notes):
Scale #6) B♭ Jazz Major (add ♯5)
Scale #7) C Jazz Dominant (add ♮7)
Scale #8) B Jazz Minor (add ♭7)
Scale #9) A Jazz Minor (add ♭6)
Scale #11) D♭ Jazz Minor (add ♯11)

Added Tone "Jazz" Scales (Nine notes):
Scale #12) C Jazz Dominant (add ♭3 and ♮7)
Scale #13) C Jazz Major (add ♭3 and ♭6)

Symmetrical Scales:
Scale #5) G♯ Diminished - 1/2,1,1/2,1,1/2,1, etc.
Scale #10) Symmetrical - 1/2,1/2,1 1/2,1/2,1, etc.
Scale #15) Whole Tone - 1,1,1,1,1,1, etc.

Scale #1: C major, D minor, G7

This first scale is C major, and it is most commonly used over C, Dm7 and G7. This is a seven note scale and is often given seven different names, one for each starting note. For example: ionian (C-C), dorian (D-D), phrygian (E-E), lydian (F-F), mixolydian (G-G), aeolian (A-A) and locrian (B-B). Although he is very aware of each of its permutations, Allan finds it simpler, and more to the point, to think of this as one scale with seven possible tonal centers rather than seven different modes.

Allan usually thinks of this scale as being related to the II chord (Dm9,♮6 in the key of C) - the chord over which he most often uses this scale.

This scale is built on the interval pattern: whole step, whole step, half step, whole step, whole step, whole step, half step or 1-1-1/2-1-1-1-1/2. The C major scale contains the notes: C D E F G A B C.

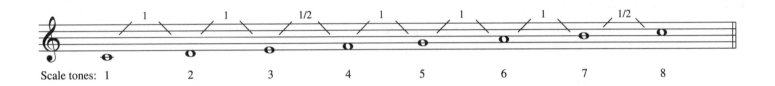

Scale tones: 1   2   3   4   5   6   7   8

The three most common chords derived from this scale are: Cmaj7(6,9), Dm7(6,9,11), and G7(9,11,13). (Available extensions are shown in parenthesis.)

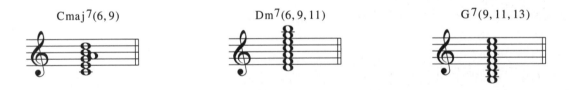

$Cmaj^7(6,9)$ $Dm^7(6,9,11)$ $G^7(9,11,13)$

Scale Diagram:

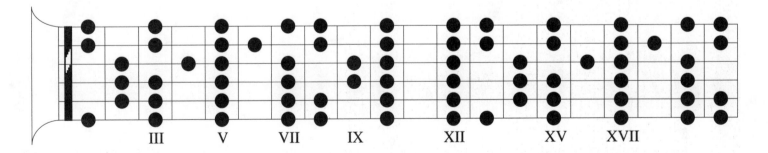

III   V   VII   IX   XII   XV   XVII

Once mastered, this pattern (and all of the following scale patterns) should be transposed to all keys.

Example 1:

A good way to begin practicing scales is to play more than three notes per string. This first example transposes the major scale pattern to F major and uses a four note per string pattern that spans the entire neck of the guitar.

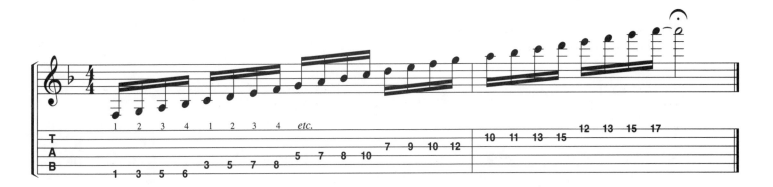

Example 2:

Allan prefers to look at the fingerboard in its entirety rather than breaking it down into separate positions. This next example is only one of many that you should develop to break out of position playing and get comfortable with entire neck.

The following pattern is played entirely in the key of C. It consists of a three note per string pattern played on string-sets 6-4, 5-3, 4-2, 3-1. Notice the finger stretches and large interval skips.

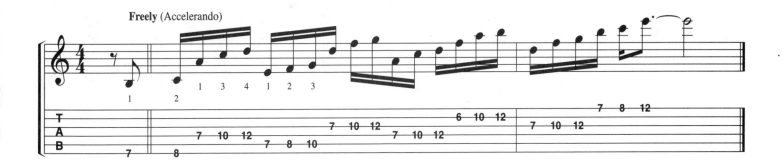

Scale #2: D minor (maj7)

This is a D minor (maj7) scale, also known as D melodic minor. This is a very commonly used scale in jazz. It follows the interval pattern: 1-1/2-1-1-1-1-1/2, and contains the notes: D E F G A B C# D.

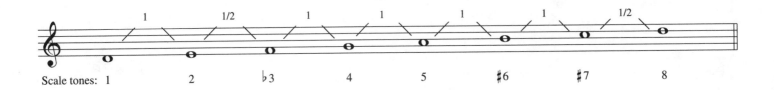

Some of the more common chords derived from this scale are: Dm(6,#7), A7(9,11,#5), G7(9,#11), and C#7(#9,♭9,#5,♭5). (Available extensions are shown in parenthesis.)

Scale Diagram:

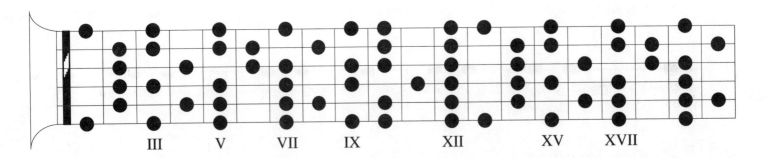

Scale #3: A minor (maj7, ♭6)

Allan refers to this scale as A minor (maj7,♭6). You can see at this point that Allan names scales by their interval relationships. This scale is often called A harmonic minor. It is built on the interval sequence: 1-1/2-1-1-1/2-1 and 1/2-1/2, and contains the notes: A B C D E F G♯ A.

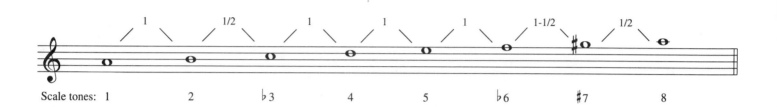

Some of the more common chords derived from this scale are: Am9(♯7) and E7(♭9,♯5). (Available extensions are shown in parenthesis)

Scale Diagram:

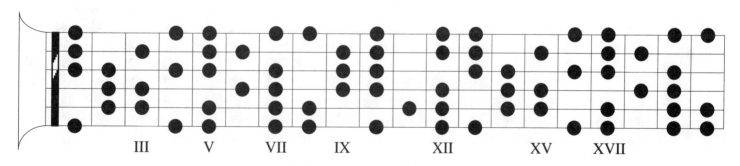

Scale #4: A minor (maj7, #4)

Allan refers to this scale as A minor (maj7, #4). It is also sometimes referred to as an E harmonic major scale (because of the m3rd from C to D#). It is built on the interval sequence: 1-1/2-1 and 1/2-1/2-1-1-1/2, and contains the notes: A B C D# E F# G# A. Notice that this is a melodic minor scale with a raised 4th.

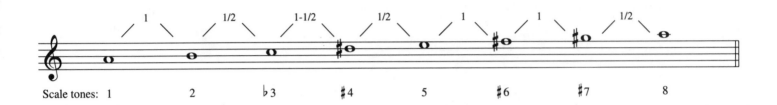

Some of the more common chords derived from this scale are: Am9(#7), Emaj9(#11,6,9) and B7(♭9,13). (Available extensions are shown in parenthesis.)

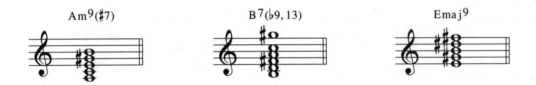

Scale Diagram:

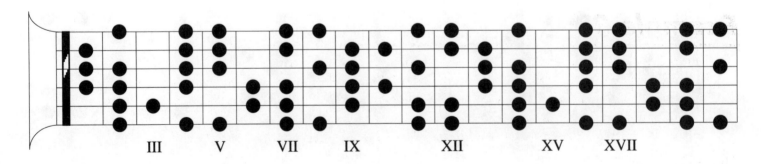

Example 3:

Many jazz players use scales like these to improvise over altered and/or extended chords (like those shown on the previous page). However, Allan often uses these scales to derive his own unique chords, around which he often writes whole compositions. The chords he derives from these scales defy traditional chord symbol notation.

This example shows how Allen used chords derived from the minor (maj7,#4) scale for an E pedal section from the tune "Letters of Marque." The chords have been numbered for easy reference.

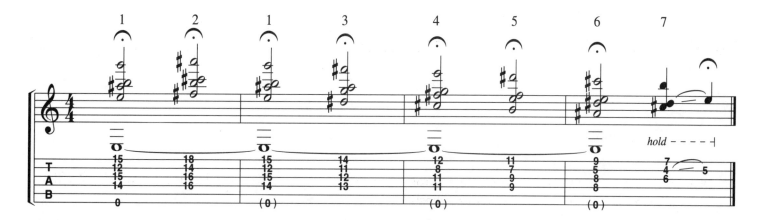

Example 3A:

Here, the scale diagram for A minor(maj7,#4) has been transposed to E.

Scale Diagram:

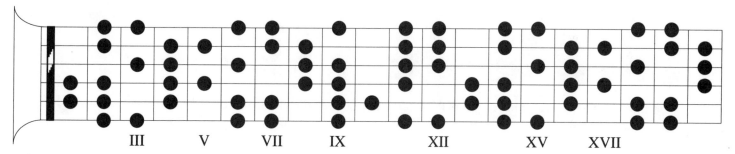

Example 3B:

This example shows how the chords in Example 3 are derived from patterns found within the E minor(maj7,#11) scale. Notice how similar all of the voicings are. Essentially, the idea is to find a chord voicing you like and then sequence all the notes in that chord voicing up (or down) to the next note in the scale. (More on this in Part II.)

Chord Voicings:

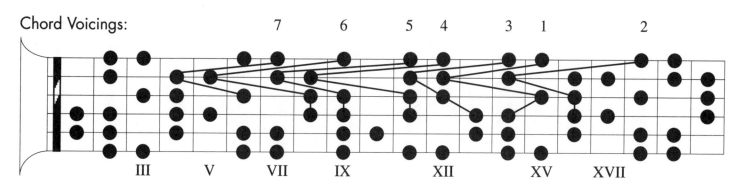

Scale #5: G# (A♭) diminished

The diminished scale is built on a symmetrical interval pattern: 1-1/2-1-1/2-1-1/2-1-1/2. Because of their symmetrical nature, there are only three different diminished scales:

    1) G# (which contains the same notes as B, D, and F
diminished),

    2) A (which contains the same notes as C, E♭, and G♭
diminished),

    3) B♭ (which contains the same notes as D♭, E, and G
diminished).

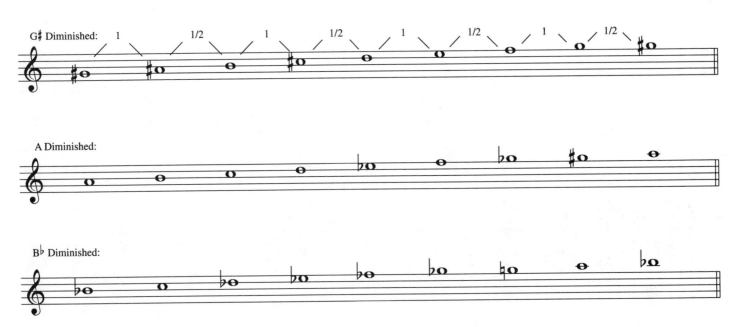

The most common usage for a diminished scale is not over a diminished chord but rather over an altered dominant chord. For example: G7(♭9) contains all of the notes of a G#dim7 chord:

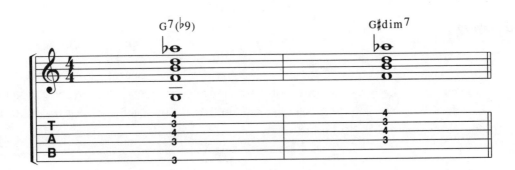

Another way to look at this would be to take the G# diminished scale and rearrange all of its notes in 3rds beginning on G. The result is a G13(♭9,#11) chord:

| 1 | 3 | 5 | ♭7 | ♭9 | #9 | #11 | 13 |

G# Diminished Fingering:

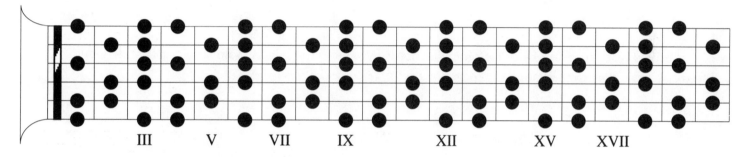

III   V   VII   IX   XII   XV   XVII

Example 4:

Inside of all of these scales are hidden chord patterns. This next example is drawn from the G# diminished pattern.

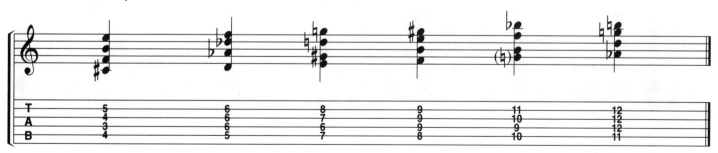

Scale #6: B♭ Jazz Major (#5)

This is the first of our "jazz" scales. The jazz scales contain added notes that work well as color tones. The most common added notes are the ♭3, ♭5, #5, and ♭7.

This scale is a major scale with an added #5. It is built on the interval sequence: 1-1-1/2-1-1/2-1/2-1-1/2, and contains the notes: B♭ C D E♭ F F# G A B♭.

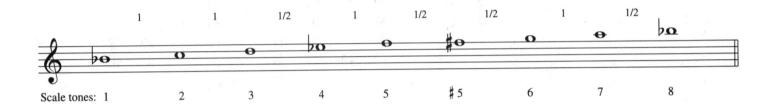

Besides working over any of the diatonic chords from the harmonized major scale, this scale would also work well over B♭maj7(#5) - also known as D/B♭, and F7(♭9).

Scale Diagram:

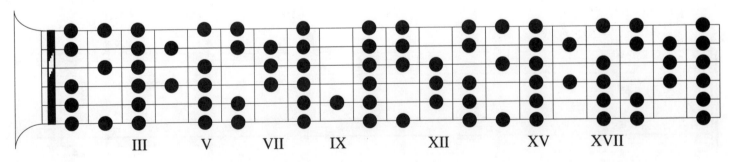

It is very important that you explore these scales thoroughly and search out different uses for each. For example, if you examine this scale closely you will see that this pattern contains within it, Scales 3 and 4, each with one added tone: G minor (maj7,♭6) with an added ♭7th and E♭ minor (maj7,♯4) with an added maj 3rd.

G minor (maj7,♭6) with an added ♭7th:

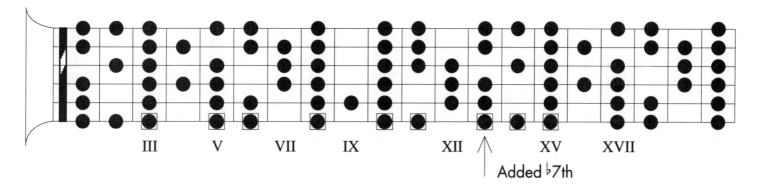

Added ♭7th

E♭ minor (maj7,♯4) with an added maj 3rd:

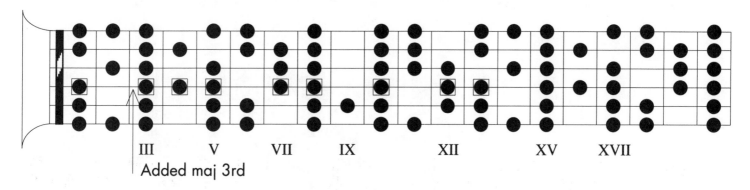

Added maj 3rd

Another important step is to examine each scale for the chords it contains. This will give you a further insight into the possible applications of each scale. For example, Scale 6, B♭ major (#5), contains the following triads: F, Gm, Am(♭5), B♭, Cm(♭5), Cm, Dm, D, E♭m, and E♭.

B♭ major (#5):

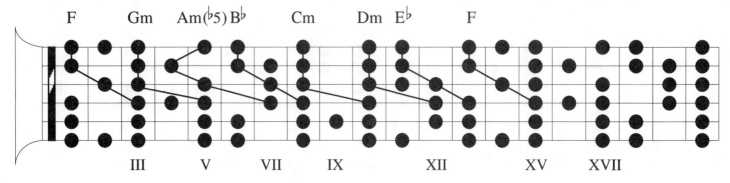

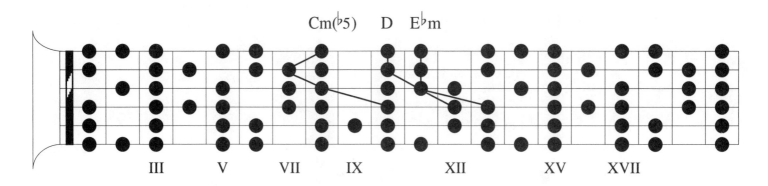

Scale #7: C Jazz Dominant (add ♮7)

This is an eight note scale, not to be confused with the standard seven note C7 (mixolydian) scale. This "jazz" dominant scale contains both the ♮7th and ♭7th scale degrees. This scale is built on the pattern: 1-1-1/2-1-1-1/2-1/2-1/2. Notice that this scale can be viewed as either a C major scale with an added ♭7 or a C mixolydian scale with and added ♮7th.

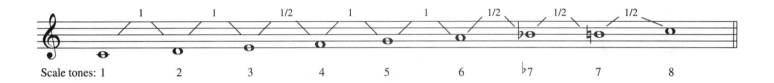

Scale tones: 1   2   3   4   5   6   ♭7   7   8

Scale Diagram:

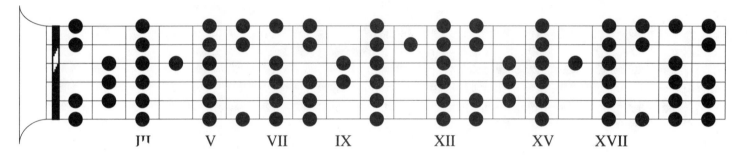

III   V   VII   IX   XII   XV   XVII

Scale #8: B Jazz Minor (add ♭7)

The jazz minor (add ♭7), like the jazz dominant, contains both the ♭7th and ♮7th scale degrees. Each of the "jazz" minor scales is the same as a melodic minor (Scale #2) with one added note. In this case the added note is the ♭7th. This scale is built on the interval sequence: 1-1/2-1-1-1-1/2-1/2-1/2. The B jazz minor scale contains the notes: B C♯ D E F♯ G♯ A A♯ B. This scale can also be thought of as a dorian scale with an added ♮7th.

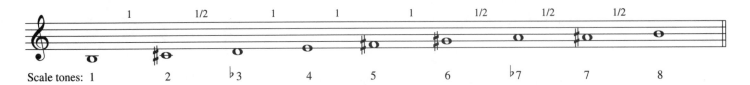

Scale tones: 1   2   ♭3   4   5   6   ♭7   7   8

Scale Diagram:

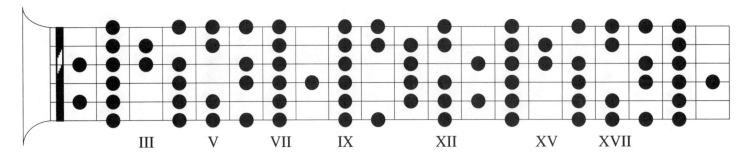

III   V   VII   IX   XII   XV   XVII

Scale #9: A Jazz Minor (add ♭6)

The jazz minor (add ♭6), like the jazz minor (add ♭7) scale, is a melodic minor scale with one added note. In this scale the added note is the ♭6th. The rest of the scale is the same as a melodic minor scale. This scale is built on the interval sequence: 1-1/2-1-1-1/2-1/2-1-1/2. The A minor (add ♭6) scale contains the notes: A B C D E F F♯ G♯ A This scale can also be thought of as an aeolian scale (pure minor) with an added ♮7th.

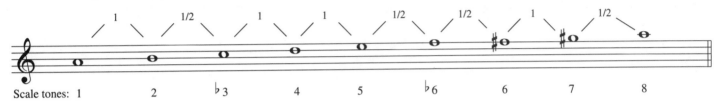

Scale tones: 1   2   ♭3   4   5   ♭6   6   7   8

Scale Diagram:

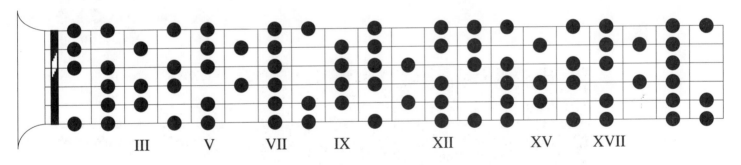

         III   V   VII   IX   XII   XV   XVII

Scale #10: Symmetrical

This next scale is a perfectly symmetrical scale built on the interval sequence of two half steps and a whole step: 1/2-1/2-1-1/2-1/2-1-1/2-1/2-1 etc. Because of the ambiguous quality of this scale, Allan often uses it as a transitional scale while modulating.

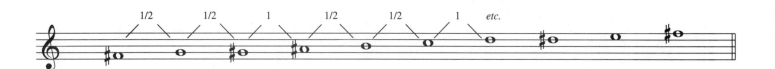

Scale Diagram:

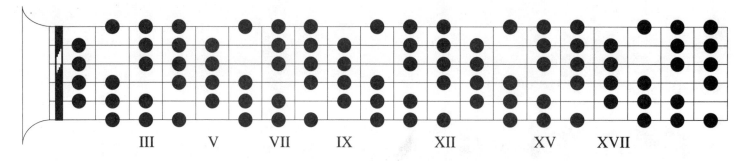

$$\text{III} \quad \text{V} \quad \text{VII} \quad \text{IX} \quad \text{XII} \quad \text{XV} \quad \text{XVII}$$

Because of its symmetrical nature, it is very difficult to say what key this scale belongs to (like a diminished chord in which any of its notes can be considered the root). Notice that contained within the scale are many chords, like C, Cm, E, Em, G, Gm, A♭ and A♭m:

C

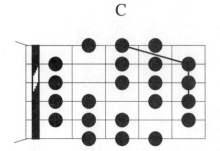

Cm

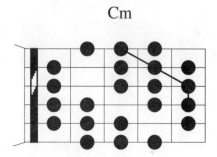

E

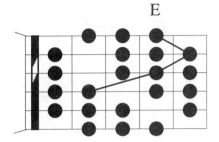

Em

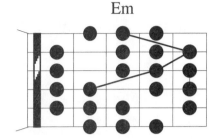

G

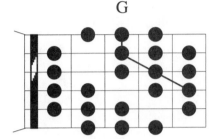

Gm

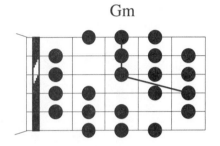

A♭

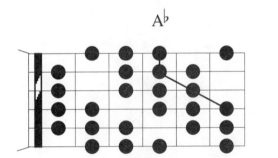

A♭m

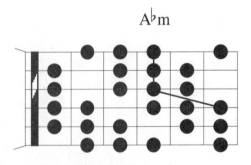

Scale #11: D♭ Jazz Minor (add #11)

(No Recorded Examples)

This is another eight note "jazz" minor scale. It is a D♭ melodic minor scale with an added #11th.

When played from its 7th degree, the D♭ melodic minor scale becomes C altered dominant. Likewise, the D♭ jazz minor (#11) scale can be centered around its 7th degree giving us C altered dominant (add ♮5). This scale contains the notes: C D♭ E♭ E F# G A♭ B♭ and C, and is built on the interval sequence: 1/2-1-1/2-1-1/2-1/2-1-1.

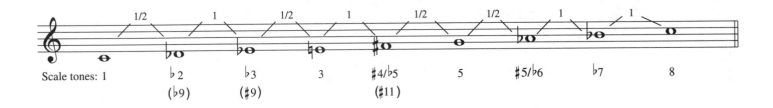

Scale tones:
| 1 | ♭2 (♭9) | ♭3 (#9) | 3 | #4/♭5 (#11) | 5 | #5/♭6 | ♭7 | 8 |

Scale Diagram:

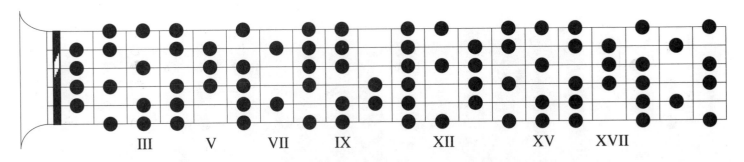

III   V   VII   IX   XII   XV   XVII

Scale #12: C Jazz Dominant (add ♭3 & ♮7)

(No Recorded Examples)

This scale pattern is very effective when improvising over dominant 7th chords. This scale, like all of the "jazz" scales contains added tones which work well as passing tones and/or altered tones over the basic chord change.

Each of the previous "jazz" scales contained one added tone, making them eight, rather than seven, note scales. The Jazz Dominant (add ♭3 and ♮7) scale is a major scale with an added ♭3 and ♭7, making it a nine note scale. The C Jazz Dominant (add ♭3) contains the notes: C D E♭ E F G A B♭ B and C, and is built on the interval sequence: 1-1/2-1/2-1/2-1-1-1/2-1/2-1/2.

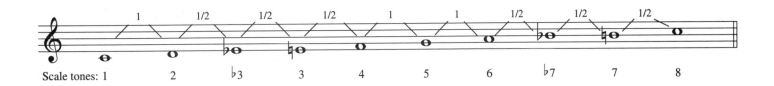

Scale tones: 1   2   ♭3   3   4   5   6   ♭7   7   8

Scale Diagram:

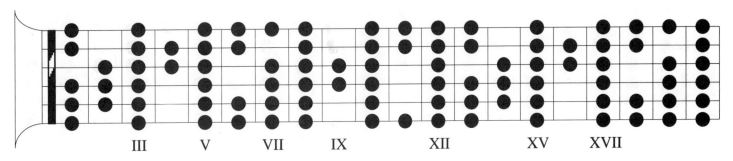

III   V   VII   IX   XII   XV   XVII

Scale #13: C Jazz Major (add ♭3 & ♭6)

(No Recorded Examples)

Here is another nine note scale. This time, the added tones are the ♭3 and ♭6. Because this scale contains no ♭7 its sound is major rather than dominant. The ♭6 is a common passing tone over a major chord and the ♭3 will add a bluesy effect.

The C Jazz Major (add ♭3) contains the notes: C D E♭ E F G A♭ A B and C. It's interval sequence is: 1-1/2-1/2-1/2-1-1/2-1/2-1-1.

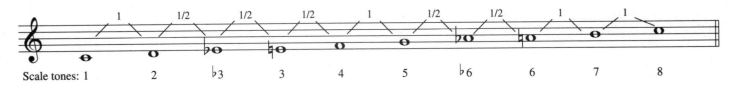

Scale tones: 1   2   ♭3   3   4   5   ♭6   6   7   8

Scale Diagram:

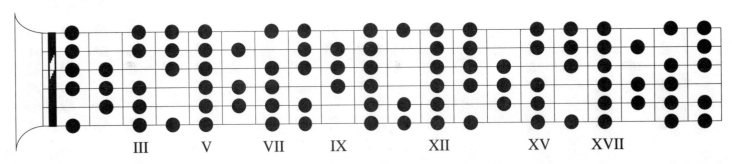

III   V   VII   IX   XII   XV   XVII

Scale #14: C Dominant (#9)

(No Recorded Examples)

This scale is essentially a C mixolydian scale with a #9 (D#) replacing the 9th (D). The min 3rd interval between the root and the raised 9th accentuates the bluesy effect of this added tone.

The C Dominant (#9) scale contains the notes: C D# E F G A B♭ and C and is built on the interval sequence: 1 and 1/2-1/2-1/2-1-1-1/2-1.

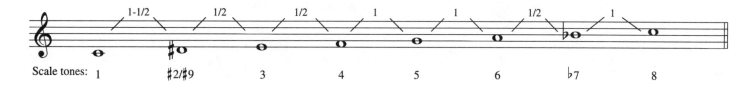

Scale tones: 1	#2/#9	3	4	5	6	♭7	8

Scale Diagram:

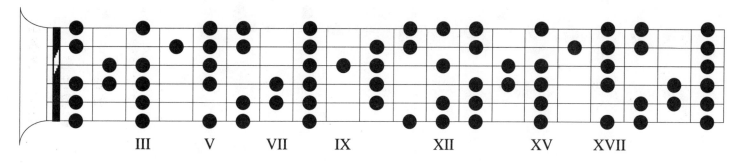

III   V   VII   IX   XII   XV   XVII

Scale #15: The Whole Tone Scale

(No Recorded Examples)

The whole tone scale is built entirely on whole steps. It contains only six notes within the octave, for example: F G A B C♯ D♯ and F. The whole tone scale is lacking three of the most important intervals, the perfect fifth, the perfect fourth and the minor second. All the scale steps are equal (whole steps) and since there is no minor second the scale lacks a "leading tone." Because of this, the scale is very ambiguous and all notes in the scale are equal, any could be considered the root.

There are only two whole tone scales, each being a half step apart from the other.

Scale tones: *Since all tones are equal, there is no reason to number them.*

The Whole Tone Scale:

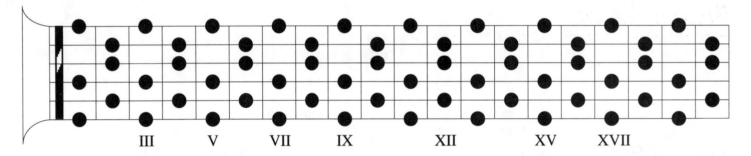

Two Common Fingerings for the Whole Tone Scale:

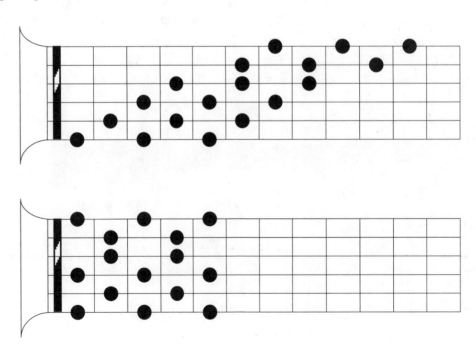

Part II
Chords and Harmony

Rather than using standard chord voicings, each chord can be viewed as being a member of a "family", the family name being the name of the scale from which that chord is derived. Any grouping of notes from that family can be substituted for the standard chord voicings (depending, of course, on your own taste and the context in which they are used). For example, if the harmony calls for an Emaj7, rather than playing a standard chord voicing (E G# B D#), various combinations of notes, all drawn from the E major scale may be used. Allan tends to play these chords in a very melodic fashion, connecting the voicings with single note lines and arpeggios. Also, the voicings that he derives often contain 2nds, 4ths and 5ths, making them very ambiguous and not easily discernible as standard major or minor chord types.

Example 6:

Here, Allan demonstrates some voicings drawn from an E major scale. Note that, except for the last chord (Emaj7), each of these voicings are derived from one basic interval shape which is then sequenced throughout the major scale. Each chord is numbered for easy reference.

Basic Chord Shapes:

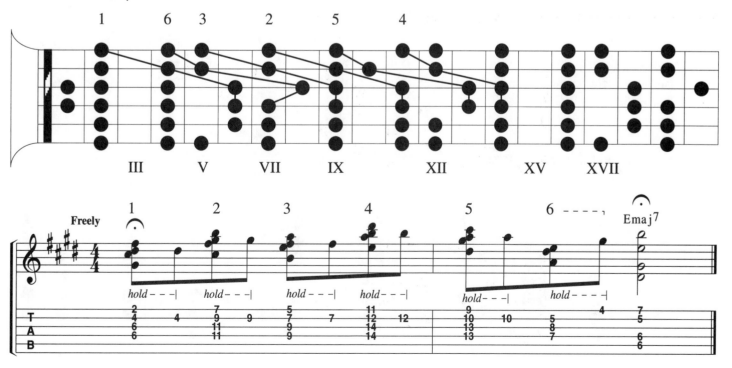

Before continuing, let's take a deeper look at this concept of harmonizing the notes of a scale to form new chordal sounds.

Coming up with new harmonizations is not as complicated as it might sound. The idea is to take a scale and find an intervallic grouping you find interesting. Then take that voicing and move each note in the chord up (or down) to the next note in the scale, finding other related chords that work well together. Because you are always using the same basic chord shape, all of the chord voicings derived from that shape will be related and there will be an automatic voice leading from chord to chord. This means these new sounds will "make sense" to the ear. This concept is not that different from the standard harmonized major scale.

Example 6A:

This example shows a C major scale. The 4-note voicing shown at the 1st fret is a standard G7 chord. By moving each note in that chord up to the next scale tone we arrive at Am7, up again and we get Bm7($\flat$5), etc. This is the basis of our standard system of harmony.

Harmonized C Major Scale:

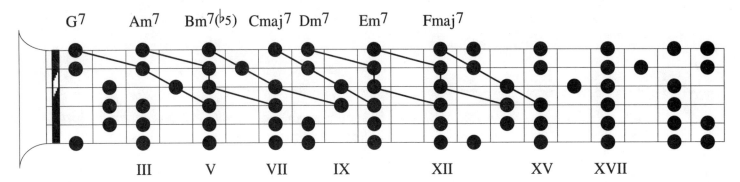

Example 6B:

Now apply the same concept of harmonization shown in Example 6A to a less traditional chord voicing (the same basic shapes shown in Example 6 in the key of E). As you can see, because we are using one basic chord shape, all of the chord voicings derived from that shape are related and voice-lead perfectly to one-another.

C Major Scale with New Harmonization:

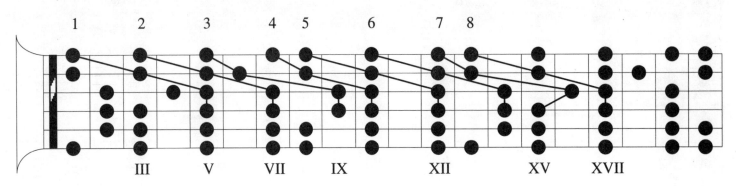

Example 7:

This example illustrates voicings that can be played over Dm7 type chords. All of the voicings are drawn from the D dorian (C major) scale. Note that all of the voicings in the first three measures are derived from one intervallic shape that has been harmonized across the neck. Note also that these chords are derived from the same parent scale as Example 6A (major) but with a different interval shape. Measures 3 - 6 have a more traditional sound because of the use of 3rds followed by a Dm9 chord.

Basic Chord Shapes:

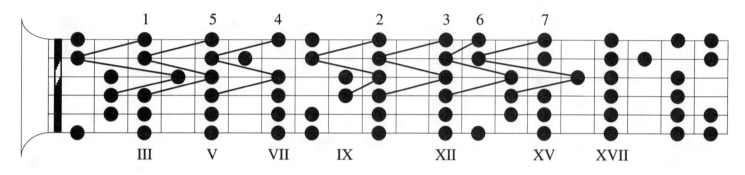

Example 8:

This example uses notes from the same "family" (major) as Examples 6 and 7, but here the focus is on creating C major sounds. Note again, that most of the chords are derived from one intervallic shape that has been harmonized across the neck (see the basic chord shapes).

Basic Chord Shapes:

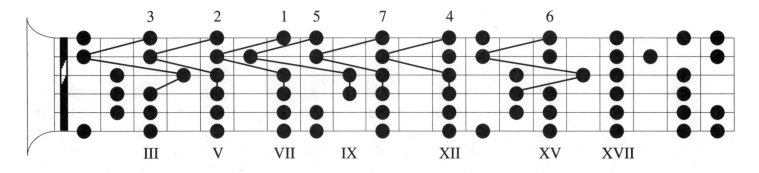

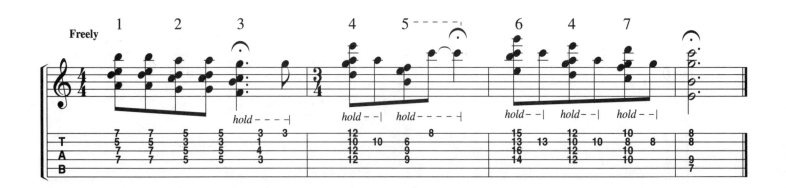

Example 9:

This example is derived from chords built on Scale 4 - Minor (maj7, #4). The tonal center is F, so the scale being used is F minor (maj7,#4). Remember, this scale is essentially an F melodic minor scale with a #4/♭5. You may want to go back and review the Scale 4 fingerings and then transpose them to F before continuing.

Basic Chord Shapes:

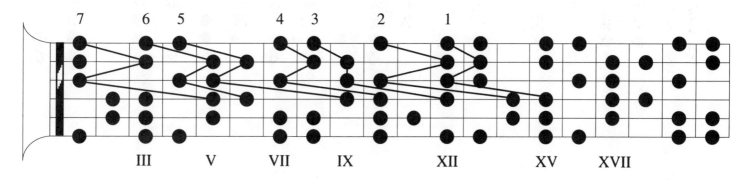

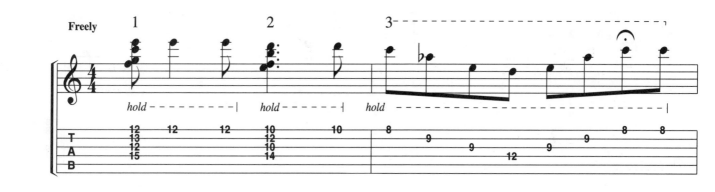

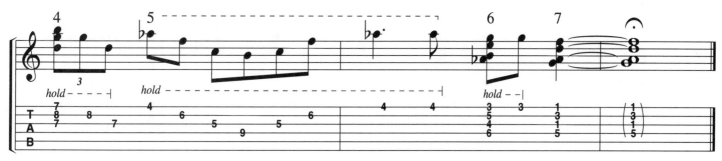

Example 10:

Here is yet another example of possible voicings from the F minor(maj7,♯4) scale. Note that, with the exception of voicing #4, all chords are derived from the same interval stack.

Basic Chord Shapes:

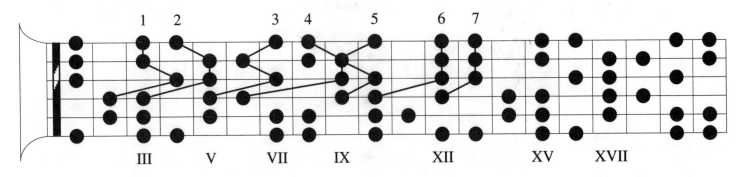

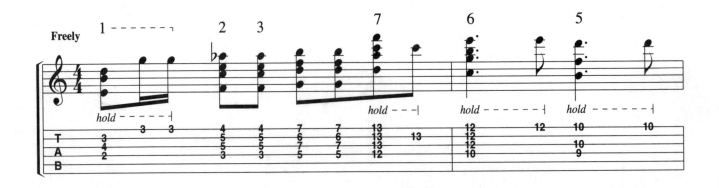

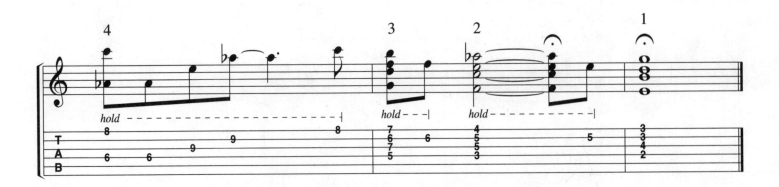

Example 11:

This example, like Examples 9 and 10 is derived from Scale 4, only this time with D as the tonal center. This example shows us yet another set of voicings derived from this scale. As you can see, the possibilities are endless. Note: The "G" on the last beat is the only note not in the D minor(maj7,#4) scale.

Basic Chord Shapes:

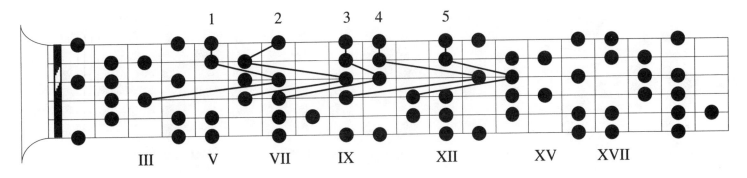

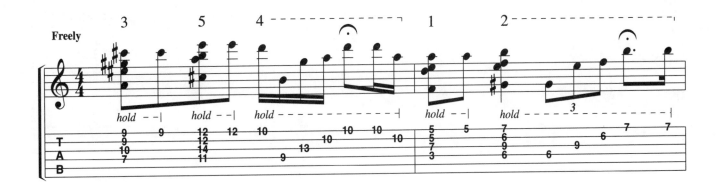

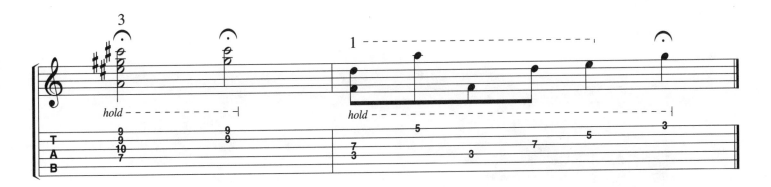

Example 12:

Like Example 11, this example is also derived from D minor (maj7, ♯4), only here the chord voicings are centered around C♯ (D♭) giving us an augmented dominant flavor (C♯7(♯5)).

Basic Chord Shapes:

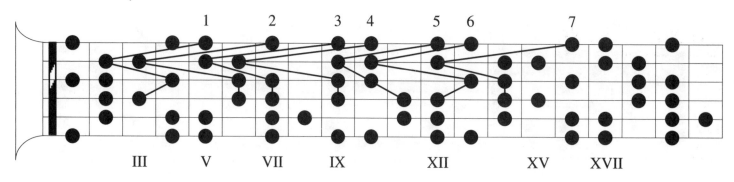

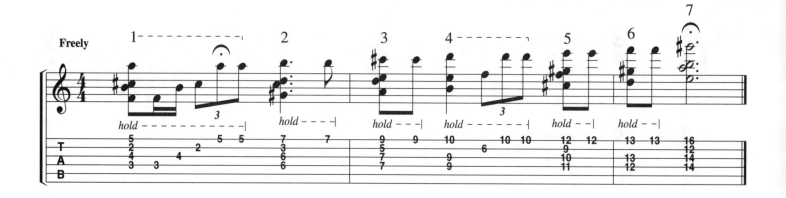

Scales with Chord Voicings

(No Recorded Examples)

Here are chord charts showing some other possible voicings for the first five scales. If you combine these with the voicings already demonstrated, you will see that the possibilities are endless. Experiment with your own voicings. When you find one you like, harmonize it throughout the rest of the scale as shown in these following examples.

Scale 1 w/Chords:

Compare these voicings to those shown in Examples 6, 7 and 8, all of which were drawn from the major scale.

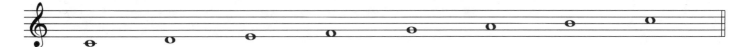

C Major, D minor, G7 Dominant:

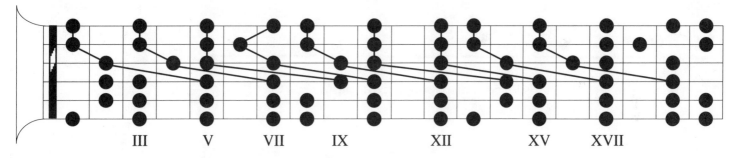

Scale 2 w/Chords:

D minor (maj7) (D Melodic Minor):

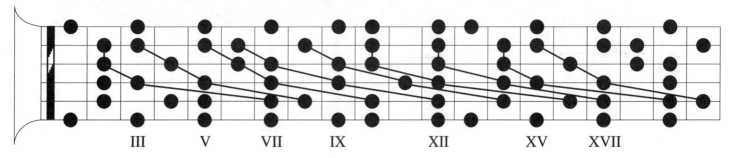

Scale 3 w/Chords:

A minor (maj7, ♭6) (A Harmonic Minor):

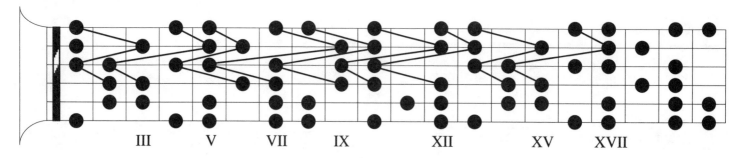

Scale 4 w/Chords:

Compare these voicings to those discussed in Examples 3, 9, 10 and 11.

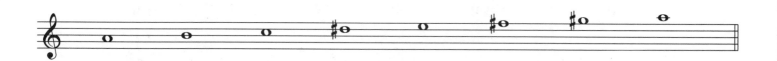

A minor (maj7, #4):

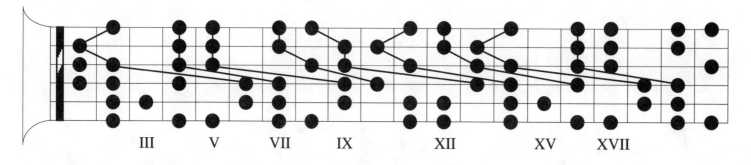

Scale 5 w/Chords:

Compare these voicings to those discussed in Example 4.

G♯ (A♭) diminished:
   (B diminished)
   (D diminished)
   (F diminished)

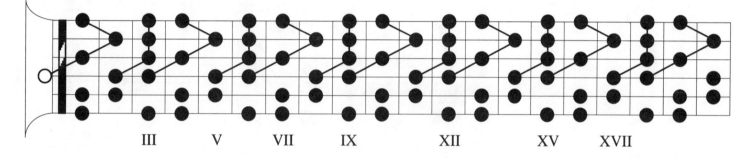

Proto Cosmos

* Chords derived from kybd. & bass gtr. parts.

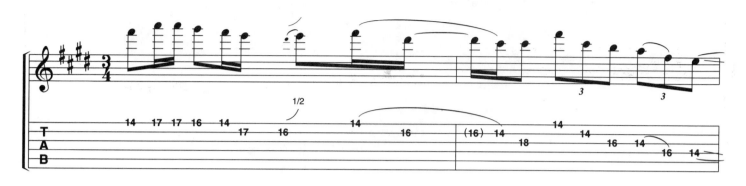

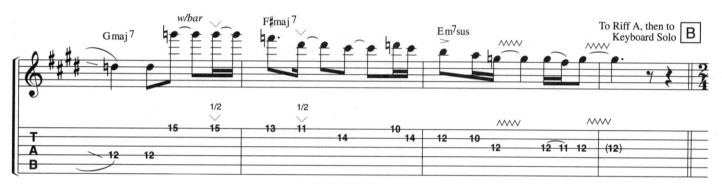

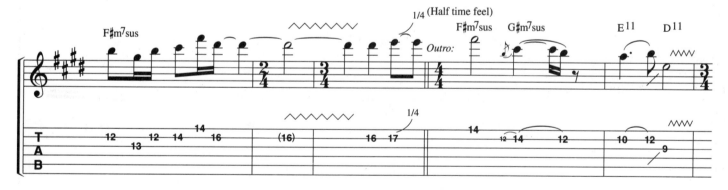

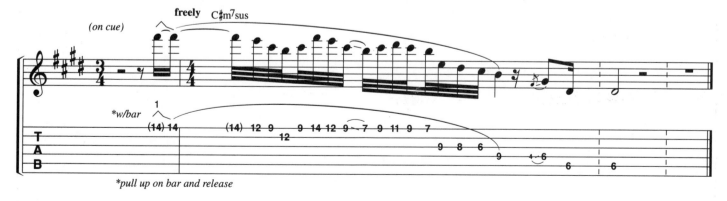

Looking Glass

Allan prefers to use different voicings for each tune, giving each song an element that is found in that song alone and is not found consistently in all the others. This gives each song a separate "color," rather than using your favorite voicings in every tune.

This song is based on very wide, open-voiced chords as shown in the following example.

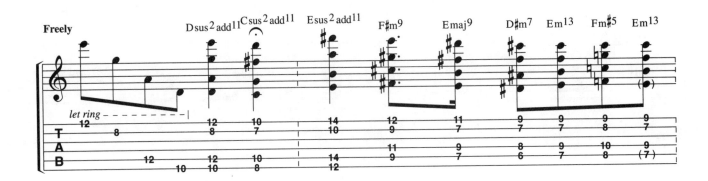

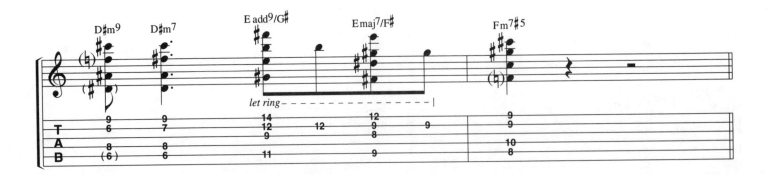

LOOKING GLASS

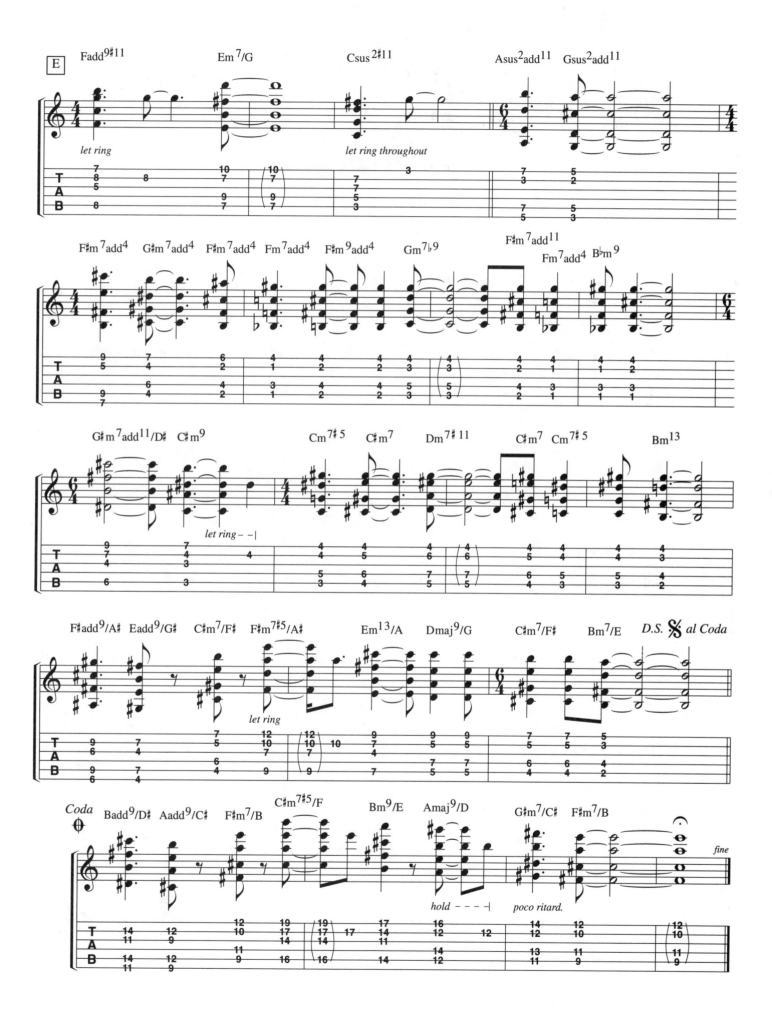

The Things You See

Example 5

Here are two examples of the basic changes to *The Things You See.*

Example 5A:

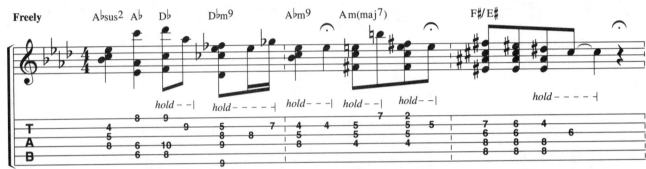

Example 5B:

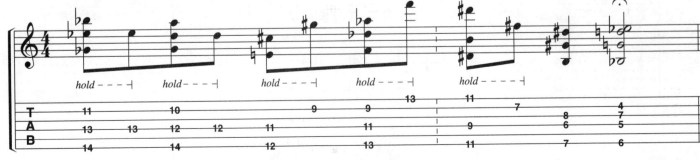

THE THINGS YOU SEE

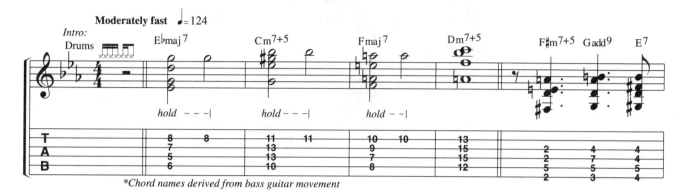

*Chord names derived from bass guitar movement

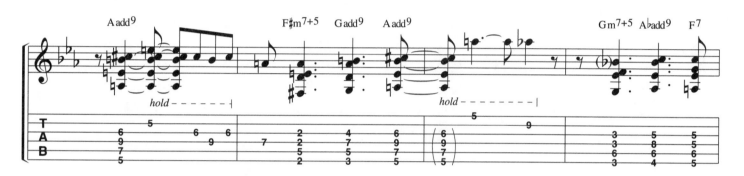

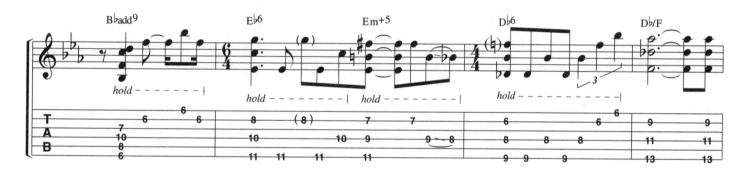

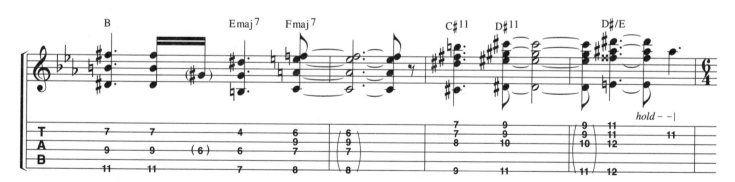

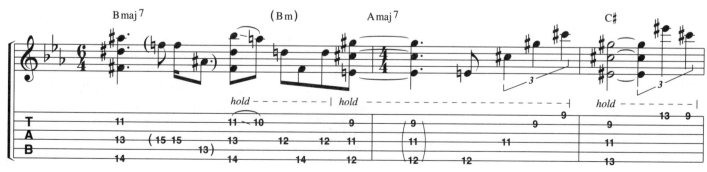

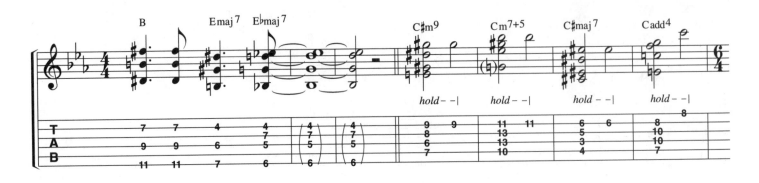

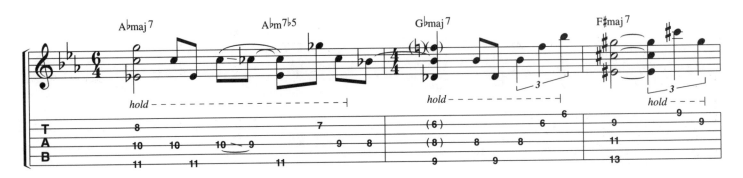

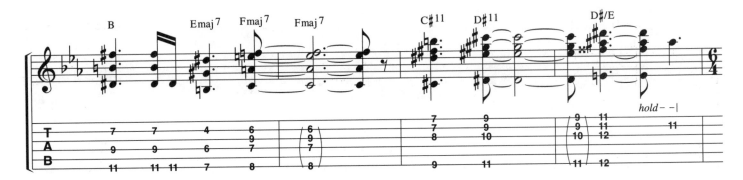

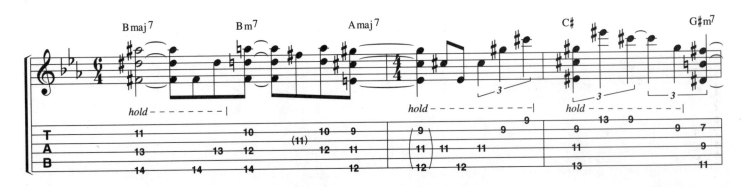

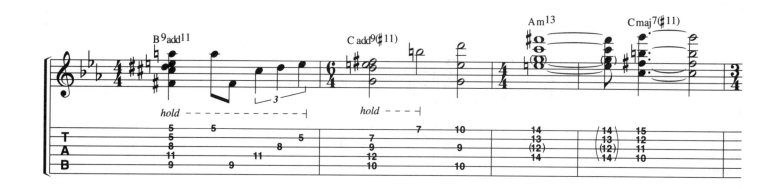

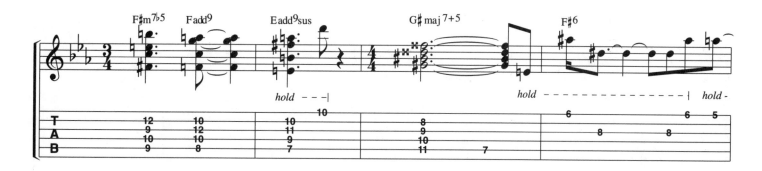

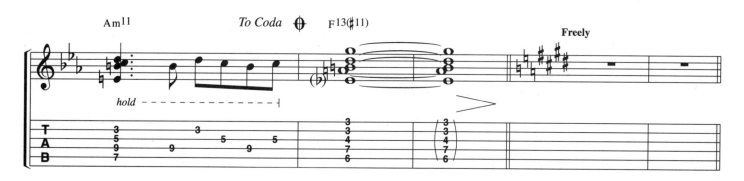

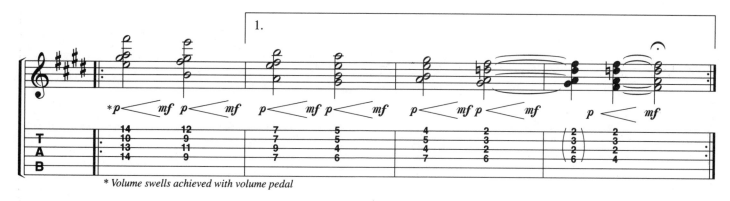

*Volume swells achieved with volume pedal

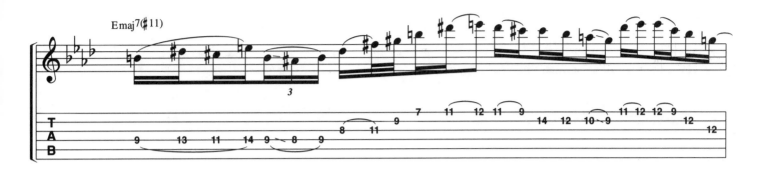

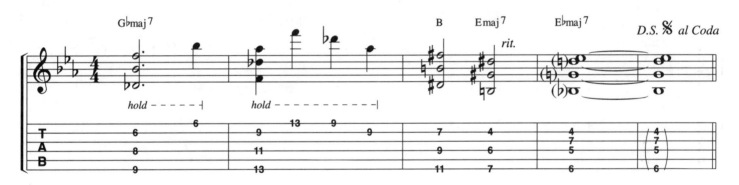

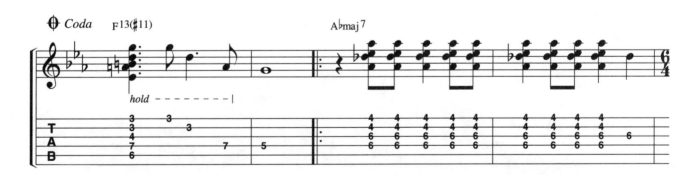

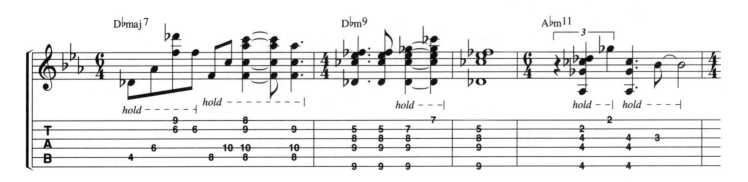

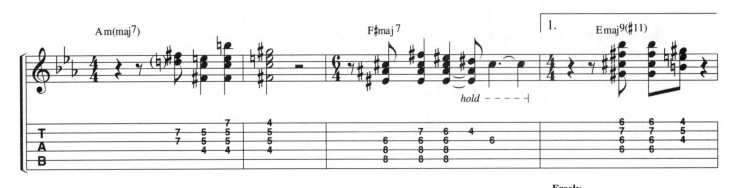

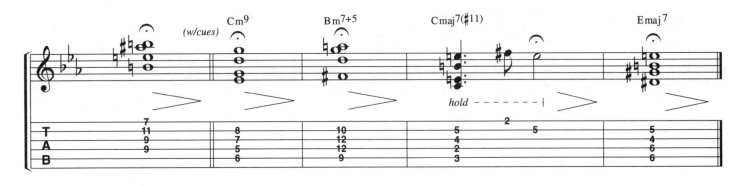

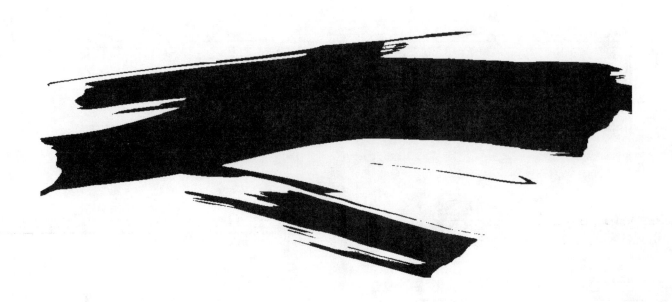

Zone

Slowly/rubato ♩ = ca.48
Clean gtr. w/ echo-delay

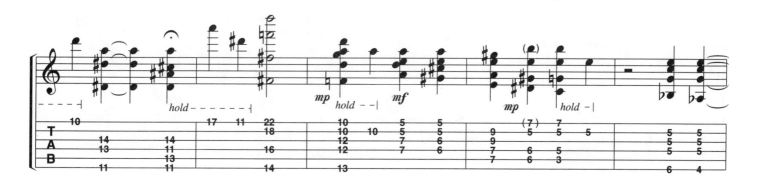

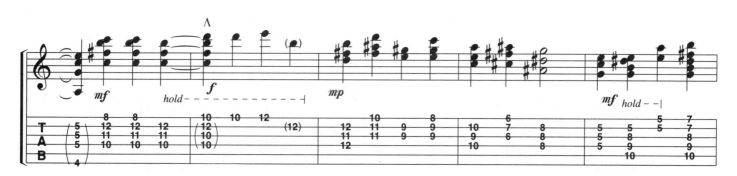

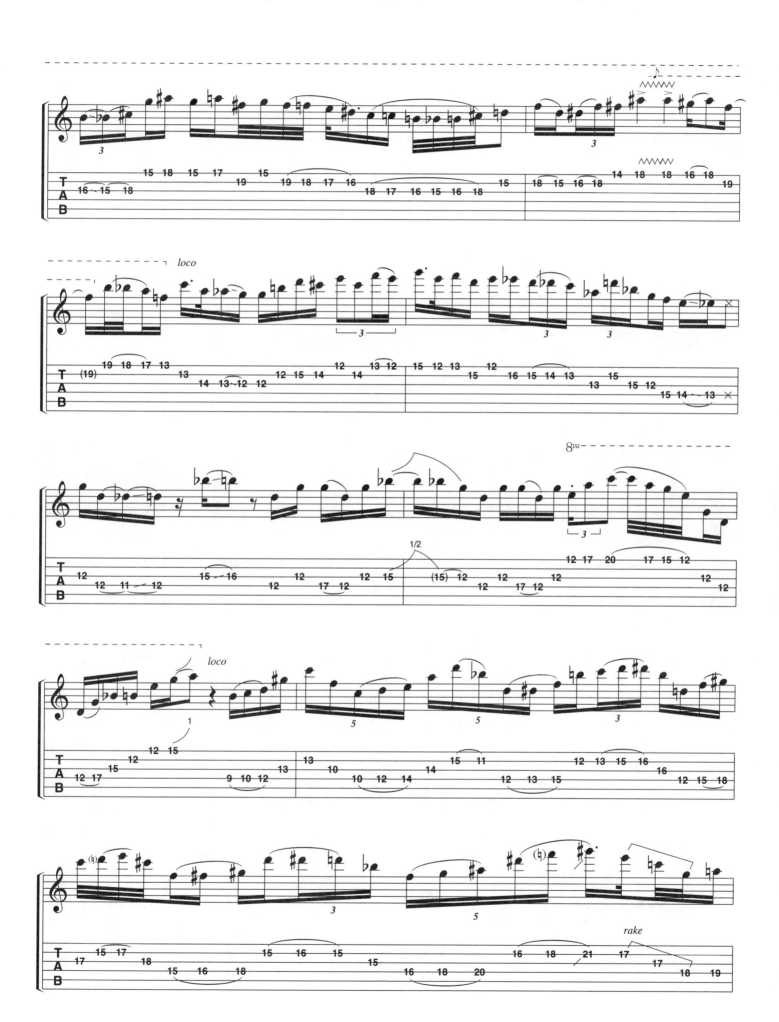

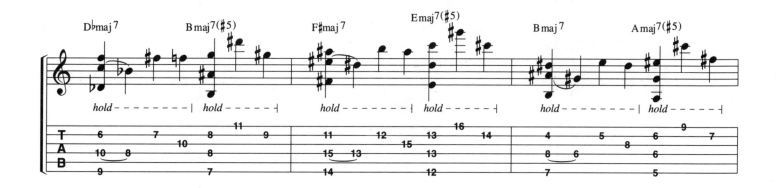

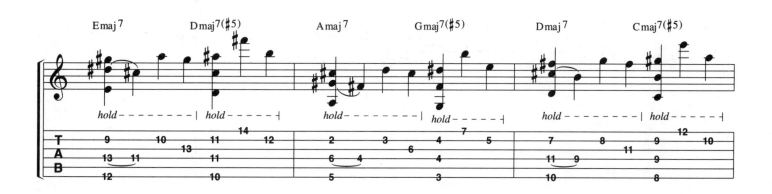

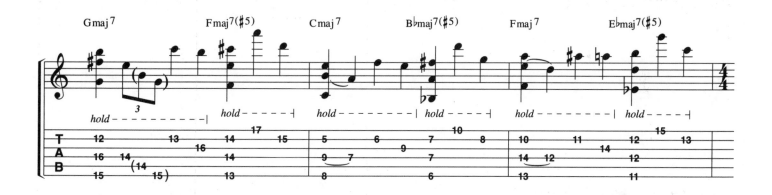

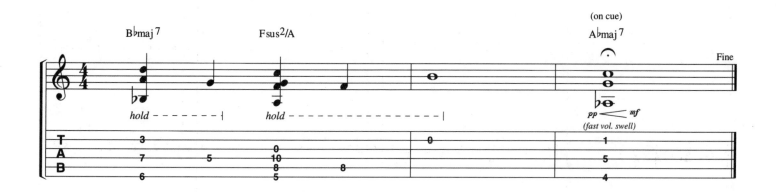

House of Mirrors

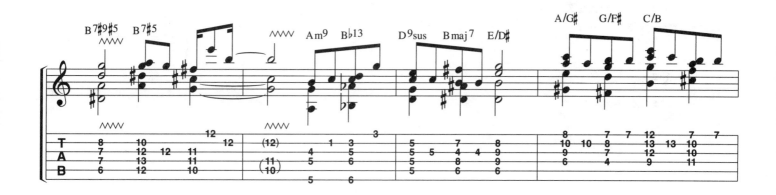

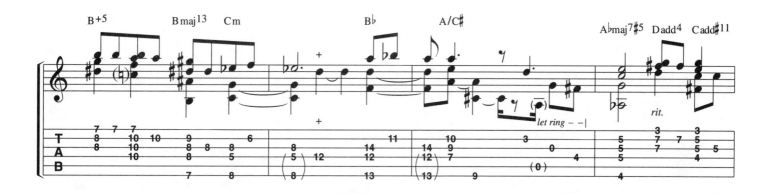

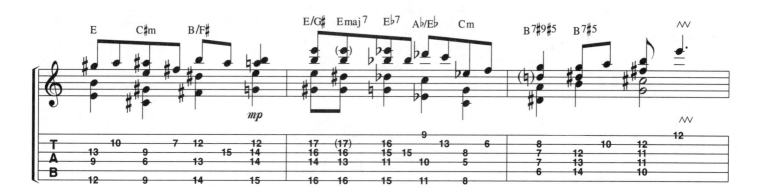

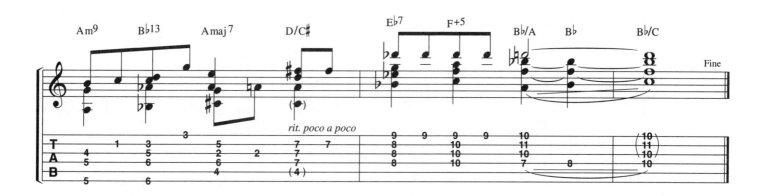

GUITAR TAB GLOSSARY **

TABLATURE EXPLANATION

READING TABLATURE: Tablature illustrates the six strings of the guitar. Notes and chords are indicated by the placement of fret numbers on a given string(s).

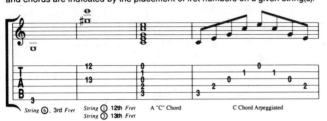

String ⑥, 3rd Fret   String ① 12th Fret   A "C" Chord   C Chord Arpeggiated
String ③ 13th Fret

BENDING NOTES

HALF STEP: Play the note and bend string one half step.*

WHOLE STEP: Play the note and bend string one whole step.

WHOLE STEP AND A HALF: Play the note and bend string a whole step and a half.

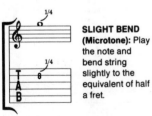

SLIGHT BEND (Microtone): Play the note and bend string slightly to the equivalent of half a fret.

PREBEND (Ghost Bend): Bend to the specified note, before the string is picked.

PREBEND AND RELEASE: Bend the string, play it, then release to the original note.

REVERSE BEND: Play the already-bent string, then immediately drop it down to the fretted note.

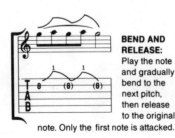

BEND AND RELEASE: Play the note and gradually bend to the next pitch, then release to the original note. Only the first note is attacked.

*A half step is the smallest interval in Western music; it is equal to one fret. A whole step equals two frets.

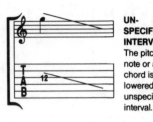

UNISON BEND: Play both notes and immediately bend the lower note to the same pitch as the higher note.

DOUBLE NOTE BEND: Play both notes and immediately bend both strings simultaneously.

BENDS INVOLVING MORE THAN ONE STRING: Play the note and bend string while playing an additional note (or notes) on another string(s). Upon release, relieve pressure from additional note(s), causing original note to sound alone.

BENDS INVOLVING STATIONARY NOTES: Play notes and bend lower pitch, then hold until release begins (indicated at the point where line becomes solid).

TREMOLO BAR

SPECIFIED INTERVAL: The pitch of a note or chord is lowered to a specified interval and then may or may not return to the original pitch. The activity of the tremolo bar is graphically represented by peaks and valleys.

UN-SPECIFIED INTERVAL: The pitch of a note or a chord is lowered to an unspecified interval.

HARMONICS

NATURAL HARMONIC: A finger of the fret hand lightly touches the note or notes indicated in the tab and is played by the pick hand.

ARTIFICIAL HARMONIC: The first tab number is fretted, then the pick hand produces the harmonic by using a finger to lightly touch the same string at the second tab number (in parenthesis) and is then picked by another finger.

ARTIFICIAL "PINCH" HARMONIC: A note is fretted as indicated by the tab, then the pick hand produces the harmonic by squeezing the pick firmly while using the tip of the index finger in the pick attack. If parenthesis are found around the fretted note, it does not sound. No parenthesis means both the fretted note and A.H. are heard simultaneously.

RHYTHM SLASHES

STRUM INDICATIONS: Strum with indicated rhythm.

The chord voicings are found on the first page of the transcription underneath the song title.

INDICATING SINGLE NOTES USING RHYTHM SLASHES: Very often single notes are incorporated into a rhythm part. The note name is indicated above the rhythm slash with a fret number and a string indication.

ARTICULATIONS

HAMMER ON: Play lower note, then "hammer on" to higher note with another finger. Only the first note is attacked.

LEFT HAND HAMMER: Hammer on the first note played on each string with the left hand.

PULL OFF: Play higher note, then "pull off" to lower note with another finger. Only the first note is attacked.

FRET-BOARD TAPPING: "Tap" onto the note indicated by + with a finger of the pick hand, then pull off to the following note held by the fret hand.

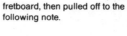

TAP SLIDE: Same as fretboard tapping, but the tapped note is slid randomly up the fretboard, then pulled off to the following note.

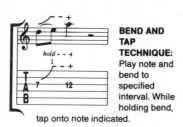

BEND AND TAP TECHNIQUE: Play note and bend to specified interval. While holding bend, tap onto note indicated.

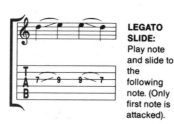

LEGATO SLIDE: Play note and slide to the following note. (Only first note is attacked).

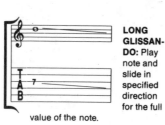

LONG GLISSAN-DO: Play note and slide in specified direction for the full value of the note.

SHORT GLISSAN-DO: Play note for its full value and slide in specified direction at the last possible moment.

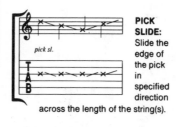

PICK SLIDE: Slide the edge of the pick in specified direction across the length of the string(s).

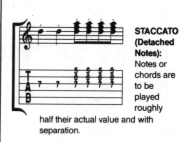

MUTED STRINGS: A percussive sound is made by laying the fret hand across all six strings while pick hand strikes specified area (low, mid, high strings).

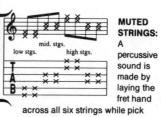
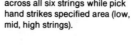

PALM MUTE: The note or notes are muted by the palm of the pick hand by lightly touching the string(s) near the bridge.

TREMOLO PICKING: The note or notes are picked as fast as possible.

TRILL: Hammer on and pull off consecutively and as fast as possible between the original note and the grace note.

ACCENT: Notes or chords are to be played with added emphasis.

STACCATO (Detached Notes): Notes or chords are to be played roughly half their actual value and with separation.

DOWN STROKES AND UPSTROKES: Notes or chords are to be played with either a downstroke (⊓) or upstroke (∨) of the pick.

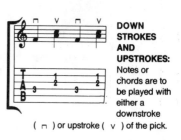

VIBRATO: The pitch of a note is varied by a rapid shaking of the fret hand finger, wrist, and forearm.